Penny Praise Ministries
Presents

Petey Pig
Celebrates
the Nativity

Written by Ms. Penny Praise
Illustrated by Lauren Hodges

WestBow Press books may be ordered through booksellers or by contacting:

WestBow Press
A Division of Thomas Nelson & Zondervan
1663 Liberty Drive
Bloomington, IN 47403
www.westbowpress.com
844-714-3454

ISBN: 978-1-5127-2063-1 (sc)
ISBN: 978-1-5127-2062-4 (e)

Library of Congress Control Number: 2015919085

Print information available on the last page.

WestBow Press rev. date: 08/24/2023

WESTBOW
PRESS®
A DIVISION OF THOMAS NELSON
& ZONDERVAN

Petey Pig
Celebrates
the Nativity

Written by Ms. Penny Praise
Illustrated by Lauren Hodges

In Loving Memory of

Sandra Marie Robertson

I know that Jesus reserved a special rocking chair on the front porch of Heaven among the butterflies just for you. I hear you singing "Blue Christmas" in the company of your red birds.

I love you, Mama.

Acknowledgements

First of all, thank you, Jesus, for my salvation!

When the Lord gave me a vision for this book, He blessed me with a whole family to bring this book into reality! Thank you so much to the whole Kelley family for working as a team in helping to bring ideas, research and artistic ability into this book and this ministry. A special **Thank You** to Lauren (and Meaghan) who spent much of her (their) first summer vacation away from college to illustrate Petey Pig's story.

I would also like to acknowledge everyone who helped bring the Petey Pig story to life in the Homer, GA 2014 Christmas in the Park celebration during the live nativity scene. Thank you Janice, Patrick, Walter, Lisa, Tony, Cathi, Leah, Lauren, Meaghan, Leigh Ann, Amanda, and especially Tate!

You are all AWESOME!!!

Dear Parents and Grandparents,

Thank you for loving your child and for sharing the love of Jesus with them. As you will see, many pages have references on them to help you and your child understand exactly where in the Bible this story gets its inspiration. I'm sure that your child will have many questions! My hope is that these references will help you answer those questions and lead to even better Bible studies together.

Petey Pig asks the same questions many children do about who God is and what the birth of Jesus is all about. As adults, we may not always take children's questions about salvation as seriously as we should. It is good and healthy for children to ask questions about Jesus. While most children spend a great deal of time leading up to Christmas wondering what gifts they will receive, this book is an opportunity to discuss with them the greatest gift of all, the gift of salvation through the birth, death, and resurrection of Jesus Christ.

So, why a pig? Of all the animals of the world, none have a worse reputation. The ancient Israelites considered pigs unclean animals and to call someone a pig is still a great insult today. But God doesn't see things the way we do. The Bible explains to us that we are all sinners, but none of us is beyond the cleansing power of God's love. We only need to accept the sacrifice of our sins upon the cross of Jesus in order to be made clean. The vision of Peter in Acts 10 reveals God's ultimate plan to save anyone and everyone who calls upon the name of His Son. Peter's vision was a turning point in the early church. From that point forward, the mission field for Christians was no longer confined to the Jewish people. Jesus Christ was recognized as the Messiah for everyone; all peoples, all nations, all sinners. He loves us all that much!

When Petey asks the donkey and sheep about Jesus, notice that all they talk about is really themselves. Their focus is not on Jesus and so they can't see Petey through God's eyes. This can lead all of us to sometimes feel overwhelmed by the opinions of others and our own faults. But Petey does the right thing and keeps asking questions.

Mr. Joshua, as a man of God, helps Petey and the others understand the true meaning of the birth of Jesus through the vision of Peter. His character reminds us to lean not on our own understanding (Proverbs 3:5), but to seek God's Word for answers. Mr. Joshua doesn't wait for Petey to accept Jesus before inviting him to celebrate His birth at the Nativity. Do you or your children have any curious friends who might enjoy celebrating the Lord with you? Don't wait for them to accept Christ before inviting them to experience His love!

There are many different crosses included within the pictures of this book. How many can you and your child count? Their placement is intentional. Discuss what they might mean in each picture with your child. This book can be a wonderful Bible study resource and conversation starter. For children too young to read, pictures are a great way to begin talking about the love of Jesus. May God continue to bless you all!

Merry Christmas!!!

Ms. Penny Praise

It's Christmas time at Mr. Joshua's Farm and all the animals are excited! To celebrate the birth of Jesus Christ, they will be part of the annual Nativity scene!

There are donkeys, sheep, cows and a family of goats. Even a flock of doves arrive to help organize this special event. All the animals are looking forward to celebrating the birth of baby Jesus – except for a family of pigs.

Luke 2:4-7

Little Petey Pig wonders what all the fuss is about. Momma and Daddy Pig tell him that the other animals are silly for acting out such a tall tale!

"Why do you want to take part such a fairy tale? Take a nice, warm mudbath, son, and soon you will forget all about it", says Daddy Pig.

"I have a lovely dinner of slop for you Petey. Your favorite! You will feel better with a full belly", says Momma Pig.

But for once, Petey doesn't want those things. He wants to know more about Jesus!

Matthew 19:23-26

Petey goes to the barn to ask the other animals what they know about the birth of Jesus.

"Why is Jesus so special, Donkey?" Petey asks.

"He is special because the Bible says it was a donkey that carried Jesus into Jerusalem!" says Donkey.

Petey doesn't understand so he goes to the sheep and asks, "Why is Jesus so special?"

"Because the Bible says that He is the Lamb of God and sheep are His flock whom He loves!" say the sheep.

John 12:14-15

John 1:29

John 10:11-15

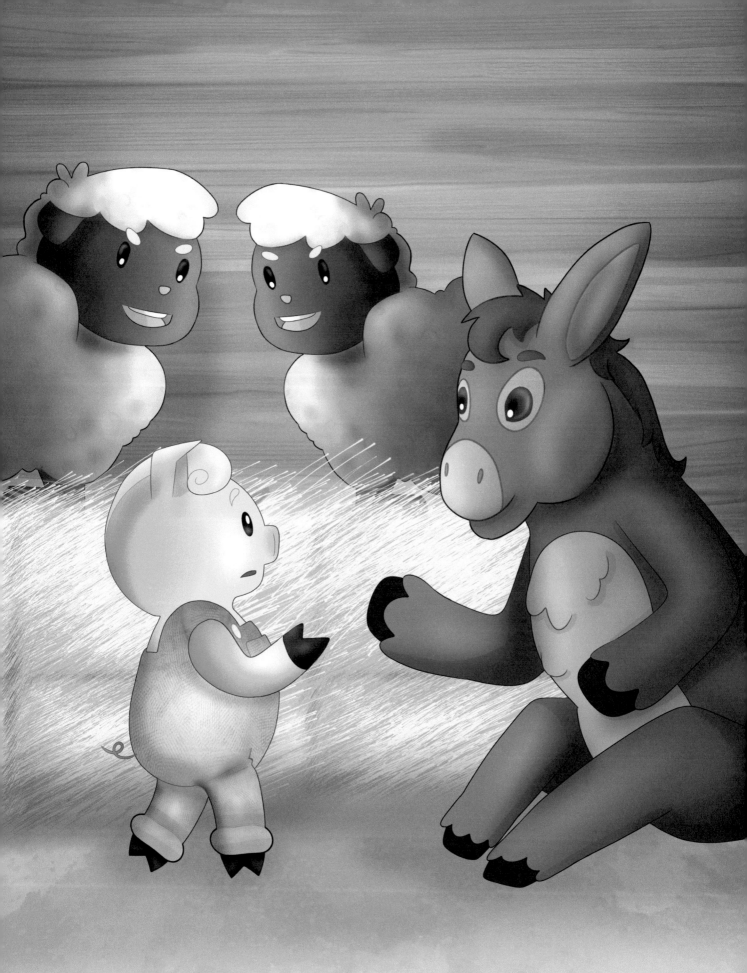

But Petey is still confused. All the different animals on the farm share with Petey their place in the Bible and why they are important in the birth and life of Jesus. But Jesus' story isn't about them, is it?

Petey asks them all where pigs are in the Bible, but nobody will tell him. He wants to be part of the annual Nativity scene on Mr. Joshua's Farm, but no one will invite him. They tell him, instead, that he is a stinky, unclean animal!

Leviticus 11:7

Finally, Petey decides to talk
with Mr. Joshua himself.

"Why can't I be part of the annual
Nativity scene, Mr. Joshua? What's
wrong with me?" cries Petey.

"Nothing is wrong with you, Petey" says
Mr. Joshua. "You are perfect just the way
God made you! And I am personally inviting
you to be part of our Nativity scene!"

"But why did they call me unclean?
I took a bath today!" says Petey.

Mr. Joshua smiles and says, "Let's go back
to the barn and I will explain, Petey."

Genesis 1:31

At the barn, Mr. Joshua calls all the animals together. He explains to everyone that God looks at cleanliness on the inside, not just the outside. To wash away the sin that makes us all unclean, Jesus was born, lived and died.

1 Peter 2:9-10

Matthew 26:26-28

Acts 22:16

In the Bible, a man named Peter had a vision of all the animals together. God told Peter in the vision that NOTHING God makes is unclean if they accept the love of God's Son, Jesus.

For the rest of his life, Peter shared the Good News of Jesus with everyone, not just the people that Peter had been taught were special to God. He learned that everyone was special to God!

Acts 10

"I want to accept Jesus and be clean on the inside, Mr. Joshua!" says Petey. Mr. Joshua smiles again and all the animals welcome Petey Pig into God's family!

The sheep make a place for Petey right next to the manger. Mr. Joshua had reminded them all that Jesus came to save everyone from being unclean with sin, not just a few. The love that Jesus has for us is always big enough to include everyone!

Acts 11:16-18

Romans 7:4

Dear God,

I believe that your Son, Jesus, died and rose again to save me from sin. Please forgive me for my sins. I accept Jesus as my Savior and I accept the new life He offers me. Thank you, God, for loving me so much!

In the Holy Name of Jesus I pray,
Amen

Welcome to God's Family!

"Whoever calls on the name of the Lord shall be saved." (Romans, 10:13)

Printed in the United States
by Baker & Taylor Publisher Services